Rupert's Tales
Rupert Helps Clean Up

Kyrja

Illustrated by
Tonia Bennington Osborn

Schiffer Publishing Ltd.

4880 Lower Valley Road • Atglen, PA 19310

Kyrja's Dedication

This book is dedicated to Jennifer L. Seney, the Pasco County Recycling Coordinator, and those who make it their life's work to protect and clean the Earth's environment.

Tonia's Dedication

To my children, Logan, Dylan, and Taylor – may you always be the Protector, the Pacifist, and the Advocate for all creatures big and small. I believe that each of you are the hope for a better world and together you will create a better future for your children's children.

Other Schiffer Books By The Author:

Rupert's Tales: The Wheel of the Year Beltane, Litha, Lammas, and Mabon
ISBN: 978-0-7643-3689-8 $19.99

Rupert's Tales: The Wheel of the Year - Samhain, Yule, Imbolc, and Ostara
ISBN: 978-0-7643-3987-5 $19.99

Rupert's Tales: The Wheel of the Year Activity Book
ISBN: 978-0-7643-4020-8 $9.99

Type set in Edwardian Script ITC/Agenda-Light

ISBN: 978-0-7643-4284-4
Printed in China

Schiffer Books are available at special discounts for bulk purchases for sales promotions or premiums. Special editions, including personalized covers, corporate imprints, and excerpts can be created in large quantities for special needs. For more information contact the publisher:

Published by Schiffer Publishing, Ltd.
4880 Lower Valley Road
Atglen, PA 19310
Phone: (610) 593-1777; Fax: (610) 593-2002
E-mail: Info@schifferbooks.com

For the largest selection of fine reference books on this and related subjects, please visit our website at
www.schifferbooks.com.

We are always looking for people to write books on new and related subjects. If you have an idea for a book, please contact us at
proposals@schifferbooks.com.

This book may be purchased from the publisher.
Please try your bookstore first.
You may write for a free catalog.

In Europe, Schiffer books are distributed by:
Bushwood Books
6 Marksbury Ave.
Kew Gardens
Surrey TW9 4JF England
Phone: 44 (0) 20 8392 8585; Fax: 44 (0) 20 8392 9876
E-mail: info@bushwoodbooks.co.uk
Website: www.bushwoodbooks.co.uk

Contents

Dance of the Dragonflies

Rupert the rabbit was far from his usual place,
Away from the meadow that was a round kind of space.

Melvin the mouse had come to him that morning,
Fretting with alarm, bringing him a warning.

"Come with me," he'd said, his eyes full of worry. "I need your help today."
Melvin didn't wait for him to answer; he just ran quickly away.

Rupert followed Melvin through the meadow and thick grove of trees,
Right through the heart of the tall cypress with their long, knobby knees.

"Hurry," he called, "there's no time to waste!"
"She'll drown if you don't really make haste."

Rupert was taken by surprise that his friend could run so fast,
But understood the problem, when they stopped near a lake at last.

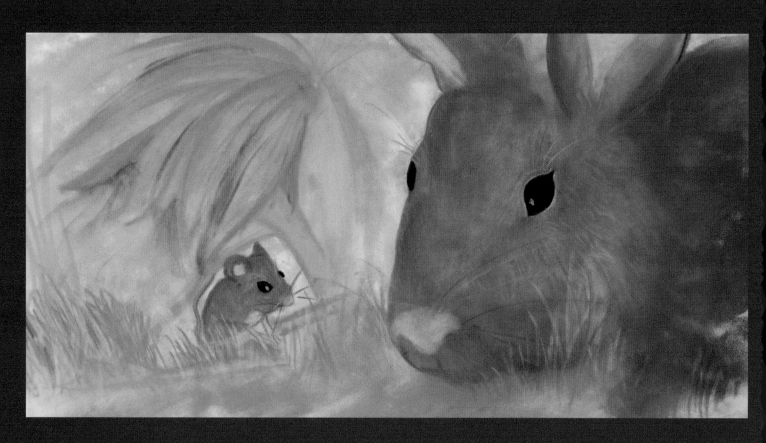

There, right near the shore, was a duck with something covering her head,
Rupert had never seen such a thing, but it filled his heart with dread.

She couldn't see anything, or even tell up from down.
Melvin was right; without his help, the duck might even drown.

From time to time, he'd seen a duck or two, once or twice before,
When they'd flown over the forest, leaving their watery shores.

But he'd never seen one close like this, and didn't know what to do.

For Rupert, webbed feet and sharp duck bills were something that were brand new.

"Hurry now," Melvin told him, "take that awful bag off of her head,"
"I'm not tall enough," he explained, "or I'd do it myself, instead."

Rupert hopped closer to the frightened duck, watching her thrash about.
He could see Melvin was right; it was up to him to help her out.

"Hold still for a moment," Rupert said, talking loud so she could hear.
She was thrashing about, squawking, and crying as Rupert came near.

"I'll take that thing off your head," he told her, "and you'll soon be all right,"
Then Rupert grabbed the thing with his teeth, pulling, and holding on tight.

The bag had an awful taste; nothing at all like grass or clover.
He spit the thing out, glad that part of the rescue was now over.

"Thank you!" quacked the duck, her big, round eyes filled with relief and delight.
She shivered saying, "That awful thing gave me a terrible fright!"

"But what is it?" asked Rupert as he sniffed at it there on the ground.
"I've never seen anything like this before, just laying around."

"I told you already," Melvin chimed in, "weren't you listening at all?"
"It's called a bag," he said scowling, "And it shouldn't be here, not at all."

5

"A bag?" Rupert asked, with one eyebrow raised and a frown
    on his face.
"But what does it do, and why is it here? Who put it in this
    place?"

"This bag is made of plastic. It's something people use for
    many things."
"For them it's very useful, but for us, disaster is all it brings."

"Oh," said the duck, "there are a lot of these bag things laying
    all around,"
"In the bushes, under the water, and just look – all over the
    ground."

Rupert looked all around, both to his left and to his right.
He was surprised and shocked to see such an ugly sight.

"I've told you," Melvin said, "people are people; they're not like
    you and me."
"They bring things with them, and then leave their garbage
    behind, as you can see."

But Rupert had seen many people before, there by his favorite
    tree.
They came and they went without ever leaving any garbage he
    could see.

They came from their homes to the forest, out in the open air,
Where they could dance, drum, and celebrate without a single
    care.

They often made fires and music and, sometimes, a lot of
    noise,
But he'd come to enjoy the times he could see all the girls and
    boys.

Not once had he seen a bag or other garbage left behind.
The people he had met had always been welcoming and kind.

Still, he could see what Melvin said was true with his very own eyes.
The people who had left this big mess behind weren't very wise.

There were bits and pieces of strange things as far as he could see.
He wondered what all the things he saw in the water could be.

Suddenly he heard an odd noise, a humming, or a kind of buzzing sound.
"Rupert!" called Melvin. "Don't be silly, you need to look up, not to look
    down!"

Rupert saw Melvin was right yet again, as he so often seemed to be,
A swarm of dragonflies flying right towards him was really something
    to see!

They made a bright cloud of color with bodies of green, purple, red, and
    blue.

The air was humming with the sound of their wings; the ground beneath
    him was, too!

"Daphne! Daphne!" he heard several tiny voices shouting with alarm,
"Come quickly!" and "Oh, you must hurry!" and "Shelly may soon come
    to harm!"

Rupert saw Melvin turn to the duck with worry in his eyes,
"Hurry, now, Daphne," he told her, "make those webbed feet of yours fly!"

"And you, too, Rupert," Melvin told him, as Daphne ran after her friends.
"Your help may be needed before this whole adventure comes to an end!"

Together the friends ran, away from the lake towards the trees.
Rupert wondered what was wrong and just who Shelly might be.

The dragonflies lead the way, weaving patterns of circles in the air,
Letting him know he was on the right track, and that he was almost there.

He didn't have very long to wait to find out Shelly was a squirrel,
That she was fond of nuts, and had a bushy tail ending in a curl.

The rest of her, from waist to head, Rupert couldn't see at all.
She was stuck inside something that was silver, skinny, and tall.

"She's done it again," Melvin said. "I don't believe it, but it's true."
"All right, Daphne," he told the duck, "you know what we're going to do."

Once again Melvin told Rupert, he too, would have to help out.
It was turning out to be a strange day, without any doubt.

The thing where Shelly was stuck, Melvin said, was something called a can;
Inside, where she couldn't reach, was a bit of food left there by man.

"Hold on in there," Melvin called out, talking loudly to the
   squirrel,
"When I tell you to push, then do your best. You can do
   it, girl!"

Then Daphne sat down on the end of the can and nodded
   her head.
"All right," Melvin called out. "Everyone do exactly what I
   said!"

"Come on now, Rupert," Melvin turned to him, "help me pull
   her out."
They pulled her tail, Shelly pushed real hard, until they
   heard her shout.

"It's no use," Daphne said. "This time the can is just too
   tight."
"We'll have to get more help or she'll have to stay here all
   night."

"No!" they heard Shelly moan, still stuck inside the can
   so deep.
"I can't stay inside here!" she said. "I'll never get to sleep!"

Rupert looked around to see there were acorns scattered
   all about.
He wondered what he might be able to do to help his
   friend out.

"Oh! I have an idea!" Melvin announced. "Everyone
   gather around me."
"There's a people place over there," he said to the
   dragonflies, "do you all see?"

"Yes," Rupert heard many voices agree, they could see
   it from the air.
It was a place that had a table, right through the
   trees – just over there.

"People?" Rupert asked, taken completely by surprise,
"You told me being near people wasn't very wise."

"Why yes," agreed Daphne, "many times you've told me
   the very same thing!"
"And me!" added a purple dragonfly. "Think of the
   danger they bring!"

Shelly twitched her tail wildly as she dug into the dirt
   with her feet,
"People aren't like us," she said, "they're not anyone we
   want to meet!"

But Rupert wasn't afraid of people, he'd seen them
   many times before,
He had often listened to their music, their stories,
   laughter, tears, and more.

"I have a plan," Melvin said. "I think I know exactly what we need to do."
"To help Shelly, we need someone big to help us, that you can all see
is true."

"Get their attention," Melvin suggested, "especially the girls and the
boys."
"Fly in circles close to them," Daphne agreed. "Hum and buzz; make
lots of noise!"

"That's a good idea," said Melvin, smiling. "Then circle back here quick."
"Maybe you should drop some acorns on them," Shelly said. "That
would do the trick!"

Rupert rolled his eyes and frowned; he didn't think that was very smart.
If you wanted someone to help, he thought, you should ask from your heart.

He was glad they left the acorns on the ground when they all flew away,
But it was hard to wait, wondering who his winged friends would bring their way.

It didn't take long to find out if their plan would work, not very long at all,
Before he knew it, there they were, surrounded by people who seemed very tall.

The dragonflies had brought with them several children laughing and having fun,
It seemed to take no time at all before Shelly was free and they were done.

He'd been afraid when he'd seen them come running over the grassy hill.
But, like Melvin and Daphne, he had managed, somehow, to just sit still.

The girls and boys who'd followed the dragonflies had seen the problem right away,
And though they'd been a little scared, they were gentle with Shelly and saved the day.

15

"Look over here," he heard one girl say, "there's garbage laying on the ground."
"And not just over there," answered a boy, "it's everywhere; just look around!"

Rupert looked at Melvin, then gave his good friend a happy wink.
They could use this help, if they knew how, if he could only think.

That's when a dragonfly crashed into him, because he was flying too low,

"I have it!" Rupert cried, "you can lead the children by flying to and fro."

"Good idea," agreed Melvin with a nod. "Fly around and lead the way."
"Then hover over the garbage that needs to be picked up and thrown away."

For the rest of the day, that's exactly what all of the new friends did —
Rupert, Melvin, Daphne, Shelly, the dragonflies, and all of the kids.

Rupert the rabbit lives near a tall tree, in the forest, and has many friends,
He's curious, furry, brown and helpful, and it seems his lessons never end.

If he could reduce, reuse, and recycle himself, I bet he would,
But that's something that you and I, as Friends of Rupert, can do and should.

So the next time you see a dragonfly, think of Rupert and look around,
Perhaps you'll see something that needs to be picked up, just waiting to be found.

Rupert and all of his friends thank you and I do, too,
For helping keep the Earth cleaned up like I know you do.

Freyan Feels Froggy

Rupert the rabbit stopped by the river to take a quick drink.
"I wouldn't," warned Spencer the sparrow, "it won't taste like you think."

Rupert sniffed the water, then made an unhappy face.
"What's going on here?" he asked. "What is wrong with this place?

Landing on a branch, Spencer turned to him and said,
"Just wait until you see what you'll find up ahead!"

Rupert looked at his friend and shook his head with dismay.
He just couldn't understand how things could get this way.

This was the same river that ran close to his favorite tree,
Right next to the thick grove of cypress with their long, knobby knees.

He didn't usually come this way, where he'd once heard there was a lake.
He was curious, and didn't always know which path his feet would take.

But today he'd been out, taking a walk, just nosing around,
And, instead of going upstream, he decided to go down.

He had only stopped to take a drink after walking for quite a while.
The grass was green, his belly was full, and the sun was making him smile.

But now, after taking one long look around, everything was changed.
Rupert even felt as though the whole wide world had been rearranged.

Seeing what lay all around him, Rupert felt sadness in his
heart.
How did this mess come to be, he wondered. How did it even
start?

For, no matter where he looked, there was garbage to be found.
Here and there and everywhere, it was all over the ground.

This was just like when he'd met Shelly the squirrel stuck in a
can.
The girls and boys cleaned up when they came to lend her a
hand.

There were strange things laying everywhere he'd never seen
before,
Bags and cans he had learned about, but here there was even
more.

Laying in the water, he saw something big and round and black.
Rupert slowly sniffed at it, then quickly took a big step back.

"No need to be afraid," Spencer told him, landing on the thing.
"It won't move or bite or even fly; it hasn't any wings."

"Whatever it's made of," Spencer said, "it's not something you
can eat,"
"But usually you find these kinds of things much closer to the
street."

"People called it a tire, but I'm not sure how it came so far."
"All I know is that people use them on their trucks and on their
cars."

"But why is that thing here?" Rupert asked with a frown. "I just
don't understand."
"This isn't a people place, and it's not part of the sky or sea
or land."

"Watch out! Oh, watch out!" he heard a distant voice cry out.
Then something ran into him and he fell with a shout.

Then he felt something slap him that was slippery and wet,
And he wondered how much worse it was going to get!

He raised his paws, then closed his eyes tight against the strange attack.
He didn't like what was happening; that much he knew for a fact!

"Stop it Freyan!" he heard a voice cry out. "Stop it I say!"
Rupert looked through his paws, then dodged quickly out of the way.

He didn't want to believe his eyes, but he could see that it was true;
There was a frog who looked ready to slap him again, a time or two.

She was smiling, as if she was happy and there was nothing wrong,
But there was a strange look in her eyes – something that didn't belong.

"Wait!" he heard the voice again. "Please wait just a minute more!"
Rupert looked around, wondering what he was waiting for.

"It's Tucker the turtle," Spencer said. "He's coming as fast as he can go."
"But if she hits you again," he nodded at the frog, " he'll still be too slow."

"What do you want?" he asked the frog, sitting there in front of him.
The frog didn't answer, though; she just sat there blinking, and grinned.

It was odd sitting there, looking at her, waiting for her friend to appear.
He couldn't help but wonder what had happened to her, and why she was here.

One moment, he had been talking to Spencer, the two of them alone.
The very next, he'd been beat up and bruised, and wishing he had stayed home.

At least Rupert thought he was out of danger, although he wasn't sure.
Whatever was wrong with her, he hoped her friend would have some kind of cure.

"There you are!" he heard a voice exclaim, as a turtle came into view.
"Do you know hard it is," he gasped and panted, "keeping up with you?"

The frog looked at the turtle, then said to Rupert, "Is he someone you know?"
The turtle – Spencer said his name was Tucker – shook his head and said, "Oh no!"

"It looks like we have a problem here," Spencer said, "There isn't any doubt!"
"I wonder what's going on, and how you are going to figure it out."

"There's a problem all right," Tucker agreed. "That is certainly true,"
"But what's wrong with my friend Freyan here, isn't something that is new."

"Can we go now?" the frog asked Rupert. "I don't like it here at all."
"We can find some shade," she said, "over there, where the grass is so tall."

But before Rupert could tell her no, before he could say a thing,
That strange, little frog opened up her mouth and she began to sing!

She opened her mouth, put her hands together, and stood on her toes.
She sang a few odd notes, then licked Rupert on the end of his nose!

"Don't be afraid; she does these things," Tucker told them, with a weary sigh.
"I wish I didn't know the reason, but I think I can tell you why."

"Come with me, I'll show you a thing or two; it isn't very far."
"Have you ever heard," Tucker asked, "of something the people call 'tar'?"

Rupert looked at the frog, then at Tucker, but could only shake his head.
He had a feeling this "tar" thing was something he was going to dread.

As he walked slowly beside Tucker, Spencer flew along with them, too,
He kept an eye on Freyan, though, wondering what she might say or do.

But she just hopped along with them, as if everything was okay,
Still, Rupert wasn't at all sure just how long she would stay that way.

"What has happened?" Spencer asked. "It's been some time since I've been here."
"I know there use to be a lake where the water was fresh and clear."

"The lake is still here," Tucker replied, "but now it's filled with awful stuff." "Bags, cans, wrappers, and bottles everywhere – all those things were bad enough."

"But not too long ago, people came and left behind three barrels of tar." "This is the worst thing," the turtle said, "any of us have ever seen by far."

"Tar?" Rupert frowned, many questions racing through his mind. "What does it do?" "It's poison!" answered Tucker. "It's a thick, black, terrible kind of goo!"

"But why did people bring it here?" he asked. "That just makes no sense to me!" "Ah!" said Spencer. "That's why Freyan acts so strange. Now I begin to see."

Just then, the frog's big, black eyes opened wide, then rolled back in her head.
She gasped, then fell flat on her face, and they all thought she might be dead.

But she jumped back up giggling, snorted once, and she even sneezed once or twice.
"Stop that Freyan!" Tucker scolded. "You scared us and that wasn't very nice!"

Rupert was about to agree, but his mouth hung open in surprise instead.
Because right through the grass in front of them, there was the lake, just like Spencer said.

But instead of being a place where animals and fish could live and swim,
The water was a sickly green with scum floating right in front of him.

There was a rotten smell in the air, and it was anything but clean.
The whole area was the worst thing Rupert thought he had ever seen.

"Oh no!" cried Spencer. "No wonder Freyan is sick and acts so strange!"
"This is so awful," he said, shaking his head. "This just has to change!"

Rupert looked across the lake at the barrels of tar dumped on the ground,
Everywhere he looked, everything was sick; even the grass had turned brown.

He looked down at the frog then and wondered about all of the rest.
She didn't seem so sick, but she probably wasn't at her best.

He'd never met her before, so it was really hard to say,
If she was always odd, or if the tar had made her this way.

Still, Tucker seemed to think there was something very wrong,
And no matter what, he knew that tar did not belong.

"Oh Tucker," Freyan croaked, "help me, please. You know what to do."
"I'm not feeling so good," she whispered. "Will you see me through?"

And, without another word, she fell slowly to the ground.
"Will she be all right?" Rupert asked, "Will she come back around?"

"We need to get her to water that's clean. We need to do it right away."
"She's never been this bad before," he added. "I don't know what else to say."

Together, they moved their friend to the river where the water was clean,
Away from the scum and grass that was brown, to where it was fresh and green.

If this was your story to tell, and these were your own friends,
Can you tell me what would happen, and how the story ends?

We all want Freyan to get all better, that much I'm sure is true,
But what about the rivers, lakes, and streams in the places near you?

Reduce, reuse, and recycle; you know these are more than just simple words.
These are what we can do to help our friends who are animals, fish, and birds.

We may not think of water much, because it falls as rain from the sky,
But our planet needs your help to see what's wrong, and to figure out why.

You may not dump tar in the lake or drop garbage on the ground,
But remember that what you put out always comes back around.

If you're a Friend of Rupert, then remember this in your heart:
In helping keep our planet clean, you have an important part.

Tucker, Spencer, and Rupert all helped their friend that day,
And you, my friends, can help out, too – each and every day.

Simba Says So

Rupert the rabbit was stuck in a cage made of wire and wood.
No matter how hard he tried to stay calm, there was no way
he could.

A fairy with silvery bells had come to him one bright Winter
day,
Warning him that his life was about to change in a very
strange way.

She told him to be brave and to please just sit very still.
She said a boy would come for him and take him from his hill.

Rupert couldn't believe what she said had really come to
pass.
And he really hadn't thought it would have happened quite
so fast!

How the fairy knew what was going to happen, he didn't know,
But the boy had showed up the very next day, all covered in
snow.

With his heart beating fast, he'd held still, just as the fairy
had said,
Even though he'd wanted to run far away – and quickly! –
instead.

The only one he'd ever known to leave the forest was Melvin
the mouse,
But he doubted even he had ever seen inside of a people
house!

There were many, many strange things here, and often way
too much noise!
A Mom and Dad lived in this house, along with a girl and two
boys.

Tyler was the name of the boy who had
  taken him from his home that day,
And though he was always nice to him,
  Rupert still wanted to get away!

He thought he'd surely go crazy if he didn't
  get out of the cage soon.
He'd already been stuck inside the thing
  through the rising of three whole moons!

Too, he often wished the fairy would have
  taken a bit more time,
To explain why he was here – if there was
  any reason or rhyme.

He missed his tree and the hill with its
  round kind of place,
Where all the people would come to make
  their sacred space.

Here, in this house, there was no forest
  with a thick grove of trees,
No elms, oaks, birch, or even cypress with
  their long, knobby knees.

Still, his cage was placed near a window
  and he wasn't always by himself.
There was a friendly old dog who came and
  went, and some fish up on a shelf.

The little girl, whose name was Taylor,
  came to feed him every day,
And Tyler's younger brother, Robert,
  sometimes took him out to play.

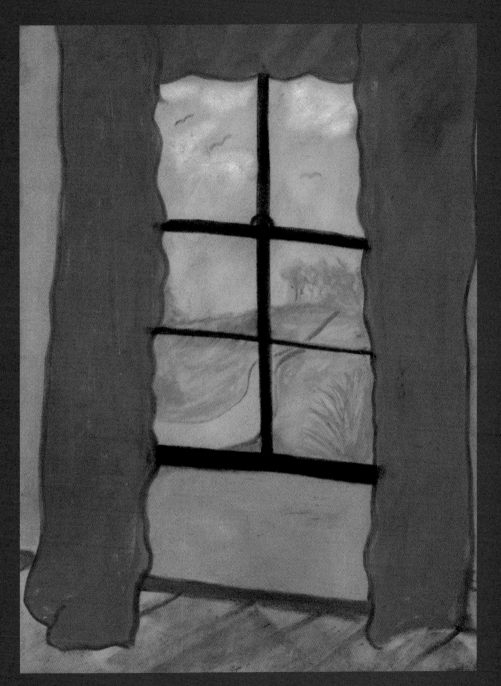

Rupert liked it when Tyler put him in his bed and talked to him a lot,
Even when he put him deep under the covers and Rupert got too hot.

But the best thing about living in the house was having a new friend.
Simba was orange and white, with a black spot on his tail at the end.

Rupert had never met a cat before coming to live in the house,
And wondered if Simba would like his forest friends, like Melvin the mouse.

Like Melvin, Simba knew a lot of things and often had much to say.
He helped to explain a lot of things, like where Tyler went every day.

School for people was certainly not something he'd learned about before.
Simba explained about vacuum cleaners, telephones, and much, much more.

For Rupert, all the noise people made was hard to understand.
All the bells, and tones, and sounds were almost more than he could stand.

But when Simba took the time to explain to him what each sound was for,
He began to understand and it wasn't quite so bad any more.

The very hardest thing for Rupert, though, was when someone turned on the light.
It made no sense to him at all why they would want to chase away the night.

When it was nighttime in the forest, he was always sound asleep.
Here, it was still dark when the alarm went off with a loud *beep! beep!*

Just like every other day, that's how this one would get started, too,
But Simba told him today, Tyler had something different to do.

That's why he was wide awake, though it was still dark, and couldn't hold still.
Simba had told him Tyler's family was going back to Rupert's hill.

Just like his friend, Melvin, the cat got out and moved around a lot.
He paid attention to the things people did, more often than not.

He'd told Rupert stories of how people act and of the places he'd been.
He knew the homes where he was welcome, so he'd go there time and again.

But there were places, too, Simba told him, that weren't so very nice.
He said where garbage was left all around, weren't places he'd go twice.

Simba said he'd paid close attention in going about his rounds,
And that people just seemed nicer who didn't throw trash on the ground.

He said he had no idea why this always seemed to be true,
Smart people kept things clean, he said, and just knew better what to do.

Rupert remembered the people in the forest that he'd seen,
And knew that when they left each time, everything was always clean.

He'd watched many of them bend and stoop and pick up things from the ground.
Other than the footprints they left, you'd never know they'd been around.

And there were many things Tyler and his family did in their house,
That would surely please and even surprise his friend, Melvin the mouse!

The thing that made all the lights turn on was something called electricity.
This was what made everything work, from the vacuum to Tyler's TV.

And while it was hard to understand why people used all this noisy stuff,
He could see that Tyler and his family enjoyed them, so that was enough.

But Simba told him that this electricity had a high cost.
And that it was much more than something called money that was lost.

Everything is connected and leads to something else, he tried to explain.
But it was all so confusing, and hard to understand, that much was plain.

It took trees and land and people just to turn on a single light,
And so many things could go wrong, if it wasn't done just right.

And there was a terrible thing called pollution that was everywhere!
It got into everything, he found out — into the ground, sea, and air!

Rupert recalled a strange little frog, Freyan, and three barrels of tar,
And how the lake she lived in was the worst thing he'd ever seen, by far!

So he was glad to learn the family he lived with took extra care,
To tend to many things around them, like the land and sea and air.

The old dog named Rusty said there were other things people could do.
"It's not just electricity they can use less of, it's water, too."

"Many people use it to cook and clean, but don't really stop to think,"
Simba told him, "that they might run out of something nice and clean to drink."

Rusty told him most water was in the oceans and more salty than not.
And some was frozen in ice caps, so that didn't really leave a lot.

People used water for some things that would never enter
    Rupert's mind:
To flush and wash and brush, and to do strange things of
    many different kinds.

One fish said water had to be cleaned, even though it fell from
    the sky,
Before it was safe for people to drink, though she couldn't tell
    him why.

All of the things his new friends told him about water made
    Rupert think.
If people didn't use it wisely, there would be nothing left to
    drink!

And that's why he found he liked Tyler and his family and their
    ways.
They took care of each other and things around them each
    and every day.

Because they did the things they did, Rupert was excited
    today.
Simba told him that he might go home, that there just might
    be a way.

Because Tyler's Mom and Dad taught their kids how to always
    look around,
They knew to do more than to just pick up garbage laying on
    the ground.

That was why he was here with Tyler, and not in the forest, instead.
His parents wanted him to learn about animals, so Simba said.

He'd brought home a chipmunk, a frog, and a blue bird with a broken wing,
But before too long, it always happened; it was always the same thing.

The cat told Rupert, just when they got to know their new friend,
Tyler always took them back to their old homes, in the end.

While he liked meeting everyone in the house, he hoped it was true.
Still he wondered, if there was something else he was supposed to do.

He'd learned a lot about people, and about cats and dogs as well,
But if there was something more he was sent to learn, he couldn't tell.

He felt sure he wouldn't be going home if there was more to do,
And he knew it wouldn't be long before he would soon miss Tyler, too.

Simba, he would miss most of all, because he'd been a real, true friend,
He'd helped to explain all the people things, over and over again.

Rupert knew he would look at people now with very different eyes.
And understood the difference between those who were and weren't wise.

The sky, land, and sea were more important than he ever knew.
He hoped more would be like Tyler and would know just what to do.

Even as a small rabbit who had no human hands or feet or voice,
He'd come to understand that everyone can make a better choice.

The sun was coming up now, and he hoped he'd soon be on his way,
He would miss his new friends, but maybe, he'd see them another day.

43

The Clever Crow

Rupert the rabbit was sad and scared, because he was so alone.
He didn't know where he was, other than he wasn't at his home.

He had been so happy at the very beginning of the day,
But at that time, he hadn't known everything would turn out this way.

He'd lived in a house, with a boy named Tyler, instead of on his hill.
And right this very minute, he really wished he was living there still.

Tyler and his family had brought him back to the forest today.
A cat who lived with them told Rupert it had always been this way.

The boy and his family often brought small animals home with them to live.
His parents said the kids had many things to learn, and lots of love to give.

But before long, the family always took their visitors right back.
At least that's what Simba had said, and he'd been a true friend, that cat.

He'd been happy living with Tyler in the house, but he'd missed his hill.
And thoughts of all the friends he'd met while living there, made him smile still.

But looking around he knew that, after all, Simba had been wrong.
This was not at all the place where he called home; not where he belonged.

He wasn't sure why Tyler's family had brought him here to this strange place.
It didn't have a hill or a meadow that was a round kind of space.

Rupert just didn't understand why they would leave him way out here.
Even little Taylor had been confused; that much had been quite clear.

"Why are we leaving him here?" she'd asked. "This isn't where he should be."
"He'll be all right, I promise," her Mom had said, "just you wait and see."

And with those few words, the children had no choice but to be content.
So after one last loving hug from each of them, off they all went.

Rupert felt his heart break as they all got in the car and drove away.
He felt a little angry too; it wasn't supposed to be this way!

Still, there was grass and shade, and the cage made of wire was gone.
Perhaps, if he was lucky, he might make new friends before long.

So he sniffled a bit, and took one more look, then slowly he walked away.
He wasn't going home, and there was nothing more that he could do or say.

Yes, he was sad all right; that much was true, without any doubt.
Now he had to think what to do; he had to figure it out.

Rupert looked all around to see what he could see; then he used his nose,
And last his ears – for rabbits can hear quite well as everybody knows.

And this time when he listened was no different from all the times before;
His ears had heard all the usual sounds, and then a little something more.

If he had been a chipmunk, raccoon, or even a squirrel, he knew,
He would have missed the quiet little voice, and the sad sniffle, too.

It was off to the left, behind him, and near a big oak tree.
But there wasn't anybody there, as far as he could see.

Still, he knew his ears were right, so he listened carefully for the sound.
Sure enough, he found just what he was looking for, crawling on the ground.

A tiny snail, hidden beneath some leaves next to the tall tree,
Was saying over and over again, "Oh, how can this be?"

She was a tiny little thing, with a beautifully round shell,
But she wasn't happy at all; that much was easy to tell.

It was strange to think, when he'd lived with people, he'd felt very small,
But compared to the snail, he suddenly felt very big and tall.

So Rupert made sure not to get too close; he stayed a step away.
"Hello there friend snail," he said. "Tell me, why are you so sad today?"

The frown on her face turn into a gasp, then she slid inside her shell.
"Oh my," Rupert said, rolling his eyes. "That didn't go so very well."

"I won't hurt you," he told her. "Won't you come out and talk to me?"
Then, knowing snails were shy, he sat down and waited patiently.

It seemed to Rupert that he waited there for quite a long while.
So when she did finally come out, he gave her a big, happy smile.

He didn't know why, but he found out that was just the wrong thing to do!
It startled him so badly, he shouted out, "What's the matter with you?"

"I see your big teeth and long, sharp claws," he heard a tiny voice say,
"You won't get to me," she said from the inside of her shell. "No way!"

Rupert began to understand, so he said, "But I heard you cry."
"I knew you were upset, so I came over here to find out why."

"Besides," he told her, "I'm unhappy, too, and thought I'd find a friend."
"But it looks like, instead, I'll end up alone all over again."

"At least no one will eat you," he heard the snail's small voice in reply.
"You're so big," she went on, "probably nobody would even try!"

Rupert knew that what the snail said wasn't anywhere close to true.
Still, it would be hard to make her see things from his own point of view.

He sat beside her quietly, and thought about the things she'd said,
Then decided, that maybe he should try to see from her view instead.

It would be hard to be so small, he thought, and to move so slow.
Snails didn't have eyes, so how would she even know where to go?

He'd known a few snails, so knew she used feelers on the top of her head,
So instead of true pictures, she could only see light and dark instead.

And she had two smaller feelers, too, he knew, that reached towards the ground.
Those helped her find food and water and dangers that might be around.

And, while he didn't think that snails were something he wanted to eat,
He knew frogs and turtles and snakes found them to be a tasty treat.

He looked around then, and could see that the little snail was all alone.
Rupert wondered where her friends were, and why she was away from her home.

No wonder she was crying, he thought, and was afraid when he came by.
"I would be scared, too," he told her quietly. "I'm not going to lie."

"Maybe you can be brave and tell me what you were afraid might be true?"
"And if you tell me," Rupert told her, "I might be able to help you."

"Why don't you want to eat me?" she asked, sounding like she was going to cry.
"It's the only thing snails are good for," she shouted. "I don't know why I even try."

"The only thing snails are good for is for someone else to eat," she said.
"Believe me, I know it's true," she pouted, finally poking out her head.

Rupert made sure to stay back from where the snail was, a step or two,
Unsure, exactly, how he could help, or what he should say or do.

"It's true what she says," he heard a voice call down from the branches above.
"She'll never be good for anything but food, no matter what she does."

Rupert looked up and saw a shiny, black crow perched in the big oak tree.
With his unkind words, the bird was being just as mean as he could be!

He hadn't known what to say to his new friend just the moment before,
But now he knew what to say, and was ready to give the crow what-for!

"I don't know what you mean, friend crow," Rupert called, looking up at him.
He didn't much like the bird gazing down at them from the tree limb.

Of course, he knew the snail wouldn't like it, if the crow did come near.
She was already so afraid and almost trembling with fear.

"Can you tell us," Rupert asked, "what good any of us might be for?
Or even why you think someone else might be worth something more?"

"Those are good questions," the tiny snail said, "I'd like to know as well!"
Rupert was pleased, but surprised, to find her still outside of her shell.

The crow cocked his head and looked down at them with one cold, black eye,
"If you'd been where I've been," he said, "you wouldn't have to ask why."

"I've seen trees and animals and people and many, many other things."
"I've been to places far and wide, where you can only go if you have wings."

"To lots of places way up high, like tops of buildings and tops of trees."
"To low places, too, and those in between – places you will never see."

"I know how things work in this world," he told them, looking down his beak.
"I know who and what is strong and also who will always be weak."

"Insects, plants, most animals and even people have their jobs to do."
"We each help nature in many ways. Why, even the weather does, too!"

"Because you've seen so much, you think you're clever," Rupert told the crow.
"But I can tell you plenty of things that you don't yet seem to know."

"My time living in a people house with those who cared for the Earth,"
"Taught me everyone and everything has a purpose and a worth."

"I learned about the water cycle, and how it's made clean again to drink,"
"How reducing trash and reusing things is more important than you think."

"Land, water, and trees to use for people things is being used up fast,"
"So people are starting to pay attention to make sure these things last."

"There are a lot of things," Rupert told the crow and snail, "that people do,"
"So that nature is made whole again and much better for me and you."

"For me, too?" the snail asked, a sweet smile spreading across her face.
"Oh yes," Rupert told her. "Every one of us has a special place."

"I suppose you may be right," the crow said, bobbing his feathered head.
"It's not what someone does that's important; it's who they are instead."

"Well, my name is Sharee," the snail said, "and I would like to stay with you."
"Even though I don't know where we're going, or what we're going to do."

Just then the crow took off out of the tree, spread his wings and flew all around.
They gasped when he became a fairy and landed next to them on the ground.

"Hello Rupert," the fairy smiled. "My sister couldn't come, so she sent me."
"She said you would learn fast, and so you have; that much I certainly can see."

"You mean," Rupert asked, "there was a reason Tyler took me from my hill?"
"Yes, of course!" the fairy replied. "And many reasons you're not there still!"

The fairy told him, "There are many things for you to learn and see."
"And many new friends to meet!" added Sharee the snail. "Just like me!"

"Follow me now," the fairy told Rupert, "and I'll show you the way home."
"And bring your small friend along, so neither of you have to be alone."

"You'll like the forest where I live," Rupert said, "with its thick grove of trees."
"There are a lot of elms, oaks, birch, and cypress with their long, knobby knees."

"And," added the fairy, "in the middle of that shady green space…"
"Is a meadow, or clearing," Rupert added, "a kind of round space!"

So the friends turned and headed together towards the sunset in the west.
Rupert was happy to be on his way to the one place he loved best.

He knew he had more to learn and would have more adventures, too.
But for just this moment, being happy was enough to do.